Meditations
FOR *success*

Meditations for Success

ISBN-10 0-9637428-0-9
ISBN-13 978-0-9637428-0-3

12 11 10 09 08 07   7 6 5 4 3 2

Library of Congress Number: TXU 569-123
Bibliography: Includes Index. Meditations, Self Help, etc.
I O' Dell, Jennifer, Author. II Meditations For Success, Title.

For more information about Visions Unlimited Press, call 800-595- HOPE or by mail P.O. Box 7886, Huntington Beach, CA 92615.

Published in conjunction with Well Behaved Women Publishing

Printed by PJ Printers
1530 North Lakeview Avenue, Anaheim, CA 92807   Tel 714.779.8484

As The morning sun breaks
Over the high mountain peaks
Another day unfolds its dreams
And although I may not be
Enlightened today,
For sure,
I'm full of faith

Urge yourself to become the best you can today. Open your mind to new ideas and sort through them with care.

Make your choices unselfishly for the hearts of others are at stake. Be kind to your fellowmen and always lend an ear, a smile, and a hand to the sick and the lame.

Take action in your life today. It may be all that you have left. Rest and take it easy, for you are in God's hands.

This book is dedicated to my children, Huntington, Heather, and Christopher, to my mother, Shirley Joan O'Dell, my father, Digger Orin O' Dell and my husband Thomas Leva.

I would like to express my gratitude and appreciation to my editor, Frances Ramsden, for her important contributions to this book, as well as the other women authors, Angela Thompson, Kelly Phillips, Wendy Hannon, Allison Taylor and Diane O'Dell, who made the second edition of this book possible.

I would never have been able to face all the adversity that was encountered while writing and marketing this book without the guidance of My Lord and Savior Jesus.

Preface

In complete awe, without reservation, we gaze with wonder and contemplation, at the order of the Universe. By simply observing nature, we can grasp insight to God's mighty power in all things, great and small.

On a brisk autumn day one might ponder the graceful falling of a mighty oak's leaves. In fall, the oak tree intuitively knows that it is time to shed the burden of its deciduous leaves. Its intricately designed flora gently tumbles down, in feather like flights, coming to rest on an insignificant piece of real estate that is defined by the surrounding concrete everglades that stretch out around it for miles and miles. The mighty oak does not balk at the small token of space afforded it for its seeds of growth and life. The grand oak, instead, rejoices in the season of its own soul. It does not look for pity or praise from other life forms. The oak remains steadfast to its own survival.

It won't be long before our grand oak tree will lay barren amidst the diminutive, arctic patch of dirt in which it rests, contemplating only the preservation of its life. Undefined by its appearance, this great tree graciously does not oppose Creation or the seasons by which its life is guided.

It is not much later in time that spring arrives and the oak experiences yet another remarkable phase of its life. The warmth of the blazing sun, enveloped in prisms of light, gently caresses the brittle limbs of the mighty tree, melting away the cold dark residues of the dormant winter season. Welcoming, after great anticipation, the warm spring air, Mr. Oak, open his eyes and lays down willingly its season of preservation and stretches out its arms towards the heavens with praise. As the grand oak painlessly unfolds the budding life within its mighty trunk, he is empowered further by the light that caresses the darkness that once, was so necessary. Buds of new growth spring forth from its weathered, torn and scorched branches. The unseen power that was once frozen deep beneath the ground in our grand oak's gnarled roots is quietly unleashed with magnificent fortitude.

And what once was lost in the darkness is now found in the sweet scents of the summer fruit that are born abundantly across the rejuvenated boughs of Mr. Oak.

Jennifer O'Dell, Author

Today

Like the start of a new year, I will begin a brand new life.

Visions – Success

Our awareness of the seasons becomes more acute as we grow older. When the barrenness of winter disappears with spring, the sweet essence of the blossoming buds and leaves, on both flowers and trees, awakens our senses.

Then summer arrives and we welcome the warmth of the sun and the long days. Our gratitude for the beauty of nature is enhanced when fall transforms the greenery of summer into the brilliancy of orange, red, and yellow colors.

Finally, the brightly decorated Christmas tree, with the pungent smell of pine and evergreen emanating throughout the house, causes us to welcome winter. And we rejoice that the New Year is coming.

And so the cycle is now complete, and we face a new beginning, as we greet the New Year. The choices we have are infinite. All the days of the year, now passed, are part of history. But we gladly anticipate accepting the challenges that will come with this New Year.

Our days are numbered. Yet, the seasons will continue their yearly cycle throughout eternity. But we, in the time allotted each of us, should commit ourselves to bettering our lives in the days ahead. We mustn't give up. Despite our mortality, we must with enthusiasm follow through and make our resolutions realities.

Today

I will imagine that the impossible
can and will become the reality.

Dreams

Like being attuned to a medley of different melodies, our conscious and subconscious can be manipulated by our thoughts.

If we hear the song of martyrdom, we live with self-hatred and self-pity. But if the majestic chords of love, hope, and faith penetrate our hearts, then the music can be overwhelmingly sweet.

These medleys empower our minds and are the keys which are readily available to open any door to future serenity.

When we arise each morning with benevolent thoughts, we find we can meditate in a more positive manner. We eliminate our psychological dilemmas and receive a clear picture of God's divine plan when we open up our hearts and seek His will. It is His plan that we must follow in order to achieve the goals we seek.

These mental images can now be translated into benignant actions. The actions of love that follow our thinking can bring us a sense of unity within our very souls as we walk serenely forward carrying a lighter load.

Today

I will take action by
following through with
each task I have set for myself.
It is by accomplishing my daily
goals that I learn to respect myself.

Habit – Behavior – Action

Building self-confidence and self-esteem takes daily action. It is by learning and growing that we come to believe in ourselves. It takes time to acquire these sought-after attributes. But it takes even less time to break them than to make them.

Every task we complete or follow through with, even small ones such as showing up for school or work, shapes the type of respect we have for ourselves. It is when we learn how to take personal responsibility for the things we do, that we learn to admire, respect, and love ourselves.

We form our behavior patterns by the actions we take. They will never be formed just by thinking about how to accomplish those self-same actions. Action is the key that opens the door to gaining self-confidence and self-esteem.

Today

I will "flip on" the
light of faith and walk
through my fears
without hesitation.

Faith

One of the biggest obstacles in life is overcoming our fear of change. Fear prohibits us from growing into mature and healthy human beings. What causes us to limit our vision is "lack of faith."

Being untouchable and unanswerable, faith is a nebulous quality, difficult to grasp and utilize for our own benefit.

However, we can often "see" the results of faith working in many areas of our daily life. Just the mere fact of our existence proves that someone or something was believed in.

And what about some of the intangible things we take for granted? Electricity is an example of a power force that most of us cannot even begin to comprehend. Most of us haven't even the foggiest notion of how the physics of light works. Yet, just by flipping a switch daily, a room is suffused in a warm glow revealing to us that we have faith in the miracle of light.

If we intuitively knew that any endeavor we pursued in life would materialize, like light when we "flipped a switch," wouldn't we seize the opportunity without any hesitation to act upon it? That is faith.

Without faith, we will always remain the same. We will not change.

Today

I will remember that is it by
openly revealing my heart to
family and friends that I gain
true freedom and happiness.

Fellowship – Friendship

Friends and family are our closest link to personal freedom. Through them we learn to love, to share, to care, and to experience the true meaning of joy.

As we grow with them we develop an intimate and healthy understanding of what relationships really mean. In times of sadness, it is the relationships with our friends and family members who will comfort us. In times of happiness, it will be these same people who will share our delight.

Our kin will always be there for us if we take the initiative and be the kind of friend or family member we would like them to be for us.

We never have to be alone in our triumphs or our tribulations. Sharing our deepest feelings and becoming closer to the people who matter most to us opens doors to success and true happiness.

We do not have to forget that we are loved by family and friends. We can, instead, share our most intimate feelings with our closest ties, knowing that honest caring will be the precursor to healthy and fulfilled living.

Today

I will greet the day with a smile
so that I may open the door for
happiness, friendship, and love
to enter.

❧ Love

It is through loving others first that we can begin to love ourselves. Learning to give of ourselves unconditionally to another human being can be a healing and self-nurturing experience.

When we lend a sympathetic ear to someone who is in trouble, or greet a passerby with a smile or, especially, when we pray for another person's health, happiness, and prosperity, we feel a wonderful sense of belonging to God's creation.

When we are faced with the challenge of life's daily trials, we must seek out unselfishness. As we develop this behavior, we will soon realize that it is in our thoughtlessness of ourselves and our thoughtfulness of others that we are afforded a greater understanding of what love, peace, joy, and happiness really mean.

Today

I will "live" in the "now." I will not
concern myself with tomorrow
or yesterday. I realize that when
I become a part of the present
moment I appreciate the gift
of serenity.

One Day at a Time

Oftentimes we complain about how much we have to do or that there isn't enough time in the day to complete the assignments at hand. What we must realize is that in performing our daily tasks we are really receiving a great deal out of life.

If we never had anything to do or never had any responsibilities to attend to then life would be very boring and useless indeed. But, most important, there would never be a feeling of pride in a job well done.

Besides, it is in the service work we do for others that we also gain "real" satisfaction out of life. We enjoy peace and serenity in greater measures when we slow down long enough to take pleasure in the moment in which we are working, instead of worrying about the end results.

We must say to ourselves, "There is a time and place for everything, and now is the time to enjoy what we are doing". There is no tomorrow or no yesterday. There is only today. We must live in the present if we are to be truly happy.

Today

I choose to succeed.

❧ Resentment – Anger

We have no time in life to be full of resentment. Too much of our existence is wasted by holding grudges against other human beings. Our future happiness will be jeopardized if we live in a constant state of anger.

Yet many times, despite such warnings, we still choose to allow these negative emotions to control our daily thoughts and actions.

We overcome anger and resentment by letting our considerate and loving nature dominate our actions. That should be our primary objective as we interact with other people.

When anger and resentments are nurtured, like weeds, they grow tenfold by the time they are harvested. Love and forgiveness are like the blossoms of spring. They bring forth sweet fruits and eliminate any and all forms of negativity within ourselves or others.

We only live once. There is no dress rehearsal. We have the choice to live in hate and indignation or love and harmony. To choose resentment and anger is to fail. To choose love is to succeed.

Today

I will remember that I too have a
purpose for being on this earth. It
is in my heart that I can find and
develop "who" I was meant to be.

Happiness

Our mortality is too fleeting and too precious to be wasted on fear, negativity, and regret. Even though we can never reclaim time that is forever part of our past, we can learn from our yesterdays. Yesterday is yesterday!

It is our tomorrows we should be concentrating our efforts toward. It is through a change in outlook, in both our hearts and minds, that our present and future services can be more satisfyingly productive. Thus, we can turn our tomorrows into what we want them to be.

We find purpose in our lives by setting goals and then doing the footwork that is necessary to attain those goals. If we feel fear trying to control our minds, we turn to God for guidance. By asking God for His guidance, we are able to create our own special place in the scheme of things, free of any fear now or in the future.

No one is going to hand us a certificate attesting to our right to be happy. On the contrary, we find happiness when we are being of service to God and those about us. We find ourselves and our hearts' desires when we focus on how we can add to life.

Today

I will accept my life as it is and choose my life's direction wisely. I will do this with the help of God and my fellowmen.

Decision – Crossroads

At one time or another, we all arrive at a crossroad where we must choose which path to follow. No matter which one we decide to travel on, it will have a dramatic impact on the rest of our lives.

Sometimes it might seem as though the best decision to make is indecision. In other words, leave it up to fate to choose the route. But this is not a solution.

We either have to face our conflicts and walk through the choices we have made concerning them or live in a state of constant confusion without direction.

Accepting our lives for what they are now, and not for what we think they should be, will assist us in making important decisions about how we would like to change. Choices are easier when we allow ourselves room for growth.

There is no time like the present to make a decision to travel on the right path towards success.

Today

I will live and let live with peace, prosperity, and healthy thoughts filling both my conscious and subconscious mind.

❧Attitude

All of us have experienced tragedies, trials, and tribulations in our lives. These unpleasant memories are retained just below the surface in our subconscious minds and tend to affect our well-being if we let them.

In order to reprogram our conscious minds and eliminate these detrimental thoughts forever, we must expend a great amount of concerted effort.

Lethargy, however, can become a stumbling block in this process. For example, by saying to ourselves, "I'm too tired to do anything about it," can cause our subconscious to cease working on ridding us of these negative thoughts.

But if we train our minds to think positively, most negative thoughts will disappear. For example, saying this thought, "Life's given me the opportunity to use my talents in so many areas that I am able to sleep less in order to be of more service to others. Every day, I celebrate that I am alive" gives us the power to change the course of our day.

We can become the master of our thoughts, allowing no past thoughts to cloud our efforts or our judgments. It is our choice.

Today

I will let go of my own little world
long enough to see the beauty and
grace which encompasses the
entire universe.

❧Gratitude

Puffy clouds are sketched in lovely formations silhouetted beneath an azure sky. Magnificent oceans, hills, forests, and meadows are spread out around us. Yet, rarely do we look up from our daily tasks to appreciate the God-given beauty of our environment.

We are generally too occupied and too involved in what must be accomplished today or tomorrow to notice what is taking place around us.

What a freedom it can be, however, if we unleash our thoughts and gaze upon the grandeur of the universe. Just taking a moment to smell the sweet essence of a rose, or to watch the graceful soaring of a kite or a far-away bird, or even to marvel at the myriad stars twinkling in the midnight blue sky can soothe our senses and bring peace to souls.

It is only when we do take the time to look beyond ourselves that all our problems seems minimal in comparison to the vastness and beauty of creation which surrounds us.

Today

I will realize that I have everything
I need. It is my responsibility to be
grateful for the inner happiness I
have received as a gift from God.

❧Letting Go

So many of us have long held on to the idea that we could propel ourselves into a position where we would be the lucky recipient of wealth, romance, and health which would inevitably lead to great contentment.

A perfect job with a high salary, a loving husband or wife, or a windfall of money are the things we tend to believe will finally make our lives complete. So miserably we trudge through life expecting our wishes to come true or fortune to fall into our laps like ripe plums, as we vainly search for this elusive happiness.

But happiness is a by-product of our service to others in all of our relationships and respective employment. True contentment can never be found in a particular job, spouse, or pocketbook. We develop a sense of peace by "letting go and letting God" and accepting the incontrovertible truth that "man proposes but it is only God who disposes."

It is quite a paradox that only when we surrender ourselves completely to the will of God, that we finally attain the happiness we have always searched for in our lives.

Today

I choose to walk in
the light with the
spiritual resources
given me by God.

❧Spiritual Guidance

It is often true that the path towards the light is through a tunnel of darkness. It is also true that during the bleakest periods of our lives we discover within ourselves powerful resources we never knew we possessed.

These resources are strength of character, courage, faith, love, endurance, tolerance, and patience. It is during the darkest moments of our lives, when we think there is no hope for us, that the light from these hidden resources shines brightest.

This profound knowledge awakens us into the awareness that the pathways to wisdom exist in all circumstances. For we have discovered that we can walk through the most agonizing moments of our existence when we use the spiritual resources afforded us because of our tribulations.

Each day of our lives, whether we are in pain or not, or in trouble or not, can be borne because we have new spiritual armor to protect us.

This is the light that we see at the end of the tunnel of darkness and its name is Hope.

Today

I will be like a river,
not like a pond.

❧ Principles – Change

Life is made up of an ever-flowing stream of events. It is like a river moving swiftly over pebbles and stones with seemingly no end nor beginning.

By day and by night there is never a time when our life stops moving. It may slow up a bit in some areas or move more quickly in others but it is always in constant motion. Even in our sleep our subconscious continues to be active.

It is important, therefore, that we go with the flow. If we don't, our lives can become like a stagnant pond with no inlet or outlet to keep it moving.

Every stone, every pebble, over which a swift-moving stream passes, can be likened to an opportunity in our own life to be carried forward. For every obstacle that confronts us enforces the reality of the ebb and flow that occurs in our own lives.

We will always come face to face with trials. It is just a matter of time. Life ends for each of us if we, like the stagnant pond, become unable to call upon God for rejuvenation.

Today

I will fuel my thoughts with
positive thinking. I know that
the desires I have to become a
better me, lie within me.

Imagination – Creation

Fire is born from a spark. Once a flame is ignited it will continue to spread light and warmth as long as we give it enough of the appropriate fuel. And so the intensity of a fire is directly related to the amount of coal or kindling we feed it and how carefully we watch it. It is quickly extinguished when we pour sand or water on it.

We can compare ourselves to that spark. When we set fire to our imagination it is possible to accomplish all sorts of things. For example, we can develop our self-worth. We do this by rekindling our consciousness by stoking our inner flame with positive, reinforcing thoughts.

We must remember that whatever thoughts we cultivate in our intellects will directly affect the sort of person we are now or can become in the future.

Our actions are the direct result of our own imaginative conclusions. So when we fuel our inner fires we shouldn't douse them with negativity. Instead, we must keep them aflame with positive thinking.

If we don't do this, we are in danger of allowing the precious flames of hope to be extinguished.

Today

I will recognize that my life
can be truly miraculous. I will
have faith that each day is getting
better and better, even if I am
too blind to see it.

❦ Patience

We have often heard the expression; "Don't quit five minutes before the miracle happens."

There are times in our lives when all seems lost; when we can find no solution to our problems; that the way we are living will never change for the better. At such moments, we must remain still and pray for guidance. An answer will always appear if we are patient.

It is during this waiting period that we should look back and remember past moments when we surmounted obstacles which seemed as difficult as the ones we are facing now. If we can't see where God has worked His miracles in our lives before, then we are most assuredly of little faith and there is no hope for us.

Therefore, I urge you, don't quit before the miracle happens.

Today

I will remember that
balance in all things is the key
factor for attaining spiritual
growth and freedom.

Harmony – Balance

When we find balance in our lives it is as though we have discovered a gateway to spiritual freedom. When we become too tired, or too emotionally involved, or we push ourselves to the breaking point, it is then we are apt to overreact in our relationship with others.

We might get angry with a loved one for no apparent reason. It might be over a mere trifle. But by losing our temper, we trade in our serenity for chaos. Moreover, we are tempted to ignore the fact that the love and understanding which exists between two individuals should always take precedence over everything else.

We all have within us a special need for acceptance from others. And although we may not realize the full extent of our own desire for love, we can plainly recognize this need for love in others.

When we allow ourselves to adopt an attitude of unconditional love for someone else, we permit self-love to guide our own lives.

Today

I will live my life in
the now. I will cease to
dwell on my past misgivings
and mistakes. I will pray for
guidance and walk with God
consciously reminding myself
that it is by His grace that
I have been blessed with the
freedom of choice.

Choice

The old pains and hurts from the past re-emerge in our conscious from time to time. And when they do, we are tempted to cut ourselves off from the world and wallow in self-pity.

If we think and behave like this, it will lead us into a state of confusion and indecisiveness where our whole attitude and outlook on life, be it for a day, a week, a month or even a year, is in danger of being permanently damaged.

We have a choice when we encounter emotional episodes caused from our past mistakes. We can be courageous and face them with the help of God's strength. The purpose of trials, in our past or present, is to change our behavior and attitudes and see God's presence in all circumstances, especially in our own painful experiences. We must not allow our past misgivings spoil our today and our tomorrows.

It is up to us. If it is peace of mind we are seeking, then we must face our pain and walk through it to the other side. By doing this we prove to ourselves that living a life based on fear is no longer the life we wish to lead.

By changing our behavior patterns, through faith and prayer, we move forward, basing our thoughts and actions on today's decisions rather than on yesterday's failures.

Today

I will dress for success.

❧ Appearance – Physical Fitness

Our physical appearance is a definite statement of identity. If we dress shabbily or flashily we will be treated accordingly. It is the old story of "first impressions" being the most important element in our dealings with others.

But what is also interesting is that even our own attitudes and actions are directly influenced by the way we dress. We feel better when we look better. When we are proud of our appearance, we walk with our heads held high. We even express ourselves with more confidence.

We find we receive more respect from others when we dress for success. We are appreciated for the good taste we have shown and we will be commended for our sharp appearance, not only by our superiors but by our peers as well.

Each day is an opportunity for us to improve ourselves in even the most surprising of ways; in this case, taking pride in our personal appearance.

Today

I will remember that the map
to happiness and success is within
me. All I have to do is to follow
the course.

⊱Visions – Success

Daydreaming can be likened to a form of indecision as to where we are headed. The traffic, the roadblocks, and red, yellow, and green lights that flash in our mind, are signals on our highway of life. These warning indicators must be acknowledged and cleared before we can direct our energies towards positive growth.

We are only able to drive skillfully and safely when we keep our eyes on the road ahead. Tragic accidents only happen when we stop concentrating on what is directly in front of us or when we ignore the signs along the way that will lead us toward our destination.

Mapping out our lives before the journey begins can lessen the chances of failing to reach our destination. It is the only route to success. Our hopes and dreams can become tangible rather than remain ephemeral if we chart our course before we set off on the expedition.

Today

I will seek to win by walking along the path of life's journey with honesty as my constant companion.

Honesty – Truth

Wisdom born out of personal strife becomes accessible knowledge to be used for the attainment of riches, both material and spiritual. But wisdom born out of evil conduct towards others is destructive and can only lead to our ruin.

How proud we can be when we honestly seek the right path for ourselves, even though we might momentarily stumble if we are unfamiliar with the course.

But when we know the road well, and still abuse the privilege of trodding on its firm foundation, it can definitely be detrimental to our peace of mind.

Violating the laws of nature has harsh penalties. It is a much greater achievement to lose match honestly and seek to improve one's game than to deceive in order to win.

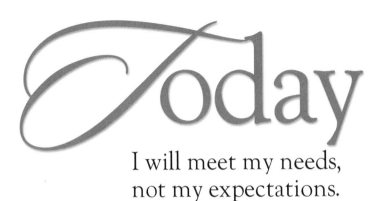

Today

I will meet my needs,
not my expectations.

❧|Expectations

Every day there always seems to be more to do than we realized. It is as though our lives were cluttered with a million and one unexpected challenges. Even though we try to arrange each day to cope with all our difficulties, still, if we feel we are unable to manage, we can become anxious and irritable. Our attitudes can decline so rapidly when we are overwhelmed that we just give up and nothing gets done.

And so, if we don't seem to be organized on the outside, it's time we take a good look on the inside. A thorough investigation of our shortcomings, and then doing something about them, will release us from the burden of trying to fix everything overnight.

Life is a daily process of solving problems. It is a process we must all learn to deal with if we are to hold on to our sanity and serenity.

We must therefore conclude from all this, that what is most important is to daily look at what is possible. If we do not succeed in our attempts at solving our "list for the day", we can remind ourselves that we are human and that we are allowed to make adjustments when necessary.

Today

It is not necessary for a tragedy to strike to let someone know I care.

Fellowship – Friendship

In times of utter despair, we cling to our natural instincts, as a shipwrecked person clings to a floating log. When we encounter unexpected dangers, our senses become more acute and adrenaline flows through us as we fight off the dangers at hand.

Unfortunately, we cannot conjure up this type of energy on command. We do, however, have the absolute power to control our emotions. And we can use our sensitive nature to build stronger relationships.

We can be like the stranded passengers of the sinking Titanic, who bonded together to set forth a strategy for survival, with no authority or preplanned organization, as their flimsy lifeboats were tossed about on the stormy sea.

We, too, can weather our tragedies best when we surround ourselves with people who are experiencing the same perils. A disaster doesn't have to precede true fellowship. In some cases, however, tragedies are necessary. This is so that we will "once more" be aware of the power that resides in true fellowship.

Today

I will take the mask off
and let the real me out.

Communication

Though our faces are painted with fear, we still believe we are showing a much brighter mask. Unfortunately, we cannot hide our true feelings forever. An insincere smile turns the onlooker off.

The "have a nice day," spoken without meaning, will not impress the person to whom it was addressed. An apology with little depth has a very slim chance of being accepted by the person who was harmed or deceived. No, we cannot fake our feelings, nor are we obliged to in any way.

The good news is that all human beings have feelings. No one is unique. It's okay to be sad, mad, glad or even had. And it's perfectly normal and acceptable to express these emotions appropriately.

The only guideline we must always adhere to is we must never hurt others through the frank expression of our true feelings.

Today

I realize that it is in prayer
that the reservoir of
hope exists.

Hope

Having hope is not just wishing for something unattainable. Hope is a humble prayer for insight. We hope our dreams will materialize and they will if we pursue life with persistence in our prayers and in our actions.

There are miracles in prayer. By the same token, wishes are but empty visions. There is hope when we don't desire mere selfish things but instead, pray for the health, happiness, and prosperity for everyone we meet; be they sick or healthy, rich or poor, sad or happy, friend or even enemy.

We see the wonderment that encompasses the universe when we find the light of hope.

Today

I will graciously accept it
as my responsibility to
be of service to my fellowmen
in all areas of my life.

Service

Sometimes we are so busily involved in our daily chores that when it takes extra effort to do something for someone else, we become irritated and feel put-upon. It's easier to say I don't want to do that; or I'm too tired; or I promise to do what you ask tomorrow.

This is especially true when these requests come from members of our own family. Have we forgotten so soon that it is in our own best interest to be of more service to others than to be self-serving?

We can get a charge out of life by caring just a little more; being there for someone else just a little more; or helping someone smile just a little more.

There is always plenty of time to do these extra services if we take the time.

Today

I realize that the unexpected detours in life need not control my attitude.

❧Acceptance

Overcoming daily setbacks can seem arduous at times. We arise in the morning feeling absolutely delighted with the day. Then we get in our car and it won't start, or at the last minute the baby sitter calls in sick. If that isn't enough, we arrive at work and it seems that a million unforeseen problems have manifested themselves onto our desk.

Generally, our reaction to these obstacles is one of; "Now my day is ruined!" We might not verbally acknowledge this thought, but chances are we're thinking it.

When we encounter setbacks such as these, we can feel more serenity when we recognize life's impediments as opportunities to grow in our awareness and seek God for His guidance. We consider the options promptly and choose the most appropriate way to implement them. When we consider and then implore this logical and spiritual tactic, our attitude will remain unaltered.

Today

I pray for guidance
of God's will for me. It's
in His Grace that I receive
the gifts of joy and love.

God

Each day we awaken to a new beginning and a new start. If we greet the morning with exhilaration, we can rest assured that we can surmount any obstacles and experiences that might lie ahead of us throughout the day.

It is when we first open our eyes that we should pray to God for guidance to do His will, not ours, throughout the day. Without this prayer, we can make a nuisance of ourselves if we are in self-will.

Every day is ours to live happily, joyously, and freely. That is a promise from God. It is our own thoughts that displace God's Grace. We have all heard it said, "Where there's a will there's a way." Verily, it must be God's will for us to be happy.

Today

I will get to know me better
that I might release the burden
of fear from my soul.

❧Inventory

We all "think" we know ourselves intimately. But do we really? Can we accept that we aren't perfect? Do we uncover our faults as well as our attributes, or are we blinded by our pride into thinking we are all powerful?

The man who sees himself as imperfect in some areas of his life has a greater chance of decreasing his limitations as he walks along the highway of success. But the man who is already perfect will remain unchanged and he limits his ability to attain riches in any form.

An honest inventory of ourselves encourages us to change and grow towards unlimited heights. When we honestly evaluate the imperfections and the attributes in our true souls and hearts, we become free from fear. We cannot be afraid of something we have already discovered has no power over us.

Today

I will put down the magnifying
glass and pick up the mirror.

❧|Growth

There are times when we lead two lives. The one portrays the chilling truth about ourselves when we stare at the image in our mortal mirror. The other life is one that destroys our capacity to forgive as we pick up a magnifying glass and tear apart another person's life with our distorted judgment.

We cripple our happiness, when we are unable to focus on our own growth, while concentrating on the destruction of someone else's life. Every day we have a choice about how we are going to think and behave. We can either nurture our inner strengths, or deny ourselves the blessings of life by haunting the path of another man's journey.

Miracles are wrought when we can let go of our judgmental behavior towards others and focus on our own destinies. Our successes, we will discover, can be uncannily sound, when we allow ourselves the freedom to accept the truth about our own journey. It is the truth that keeps our eyes focused solely on the image that is reflected in our own mirrors.

Today

I choose to reprogram my
thoughts towards creating
a happier and freer me.

Habit – Behavior – Action

As the sun rises over the horizon, we begin our day. Upon awakening, we all have a set of thoughts quickly passing through our minds. Some of them are about routine schedules; make the coffee, take a shower, feed the children, get dressed, and go to work. Other thoughts are about our new desires for the day.

We have to laugh at our robotic way of life. Even though we human beings aren't mechanical men and women, we seem to adjust our days to a particular set of standards and schedules. The only difference between the robot and us is that we program ourselves, whereas the robot is programmed by us.

When our agenda seems overloaded or unforgiving, we can remind ourselves that we have the solution to our own dilemmas. We plan our own program and we can change it any time we choose.

Our frustrations and fears are directly related to the concentrated efforts we apply to them. As we adopt different attitudes and redirect our energies, our disappointments and apprehensions fade away.

Our whole outlook upon life can be altered if we are willing to make the necessary changes. We do not have to be like that robot if we choose not to be.

Today

I will begin to change one
behavior or attitude that I am
uncomfortable with.

Principles – Change

We are reborn when our thoughts and deeds reflect our benevolent intentions. It is easier to think we can change our negative behavior later, rather than now. In other words, put off until tomorrow what we should do today.

Our benevolent intentions will come into fruition after we take the action and make the appropriate changes. There is no time like the present to begin following through with our choices.

Procrastination in daily living clouds our thought processes at the subconscious level. We will always remain guilt ridden in our minds unless we take steps towards changing the destructive patterns of our behavior. Freedom from a "guilty subconscious" begins the moment we start changing the attitudes that darken the positive side of our minds.

Productive and positive action creates constructive molds for future accomplishments.

Today

I will realize that my
need to always be right
can stand in the way
of finding true happiness.

Pride

When our opinions differ from the opinions of those we are close to, such as co-workers, children, friends, family or lovers, our pride always makes us want to be right.

It is not a simple task to stand up for our own beliefs while at the same time trying to understand another person's perceptions and solutions to life's dramas.

What a relief it can be, however, if we can learn to stop being indignant when people don't always agree with us. It is not our mission in life to be judge and jury of conflicts based on differences of opinion.

We must learn to respect another person's viewpoint even if we don't understand or agree with their positions. It is by listening respectfully to what others' think and say that we find an inner serenity. Respect from others is generated by our ability to humble ourselves.

Letting go of needless pride and anger is the first step towards achieving harmony in ourselves and in our relationships with others.

Today

I will welcome my feelings, all of them. They are mine. I will not label them as good or bad. I will realize that my emotions are what make me a whole and special human being.

❧Self-Expression

Life is a roller coaster and we all enjoy a good ride. It's fun and exhilarating when the car climbs to the top, then drops at a breakneck speed down a steep incline and finally ends at the bottom of the ride. We react to the curves, drops, and climbs anxiously anticipating the thrills in store for us around the next bend of tracks.

But isn't that why we take this ride, to feel the adrenaline flow as our excitement mounts? We like the feeling of our heart pounding. It makes us come alive, for we are living in the moment.

In much the same way, we like to believe that our entire existence should be filled with fun and excitement. But life isn't just for experiencing the high moments. We must also feel pain and sorrow and be wary of the pitfalls that stalk our path.

Life is full of contrasts. We have to know sadness if we are to appreciate joy. We have to know pain and tragedy if we are to value love and happiness.

It is necessary to express our feelings for everything, be it good or bad, sad or joyful. It is not an easy task, but if we are to become whole people, we must take responsibility for all of our feelings.

We cannot deny our true and honest feelings just because they hurt us when we acknowledge them. Pain is an important part of our individual makeup. "All" of our emotions are intrinsic elements of our beings that contribute to our own uniqueness.

Today

I will be a rock to whom-ever calls on me for help.

❧Understanding

Our hearts are touched with an abundance of gratitude when close friends or family members are facing painful crisis and they call upon us for help.

It really is not important whether their pain is physical or emotional. The foundation of our own growth will be enhanced when we can allow someone else's pain to teach us the magnitude of our own sorrows.

Being quiet long enough to hear our own silent screams for merciful relief gives us the ability to hear that same call for help in someone else and respond to it compassionately. When we are willing to search our hearts for empathy, we are blessed with the capacity to listen to someone else's painful calamity.

Although, in many cases, we are not called to solve other people's problems, we can be there for them with support, encouragement, and love, as they mend themselves with their own solutions. We become merely the rock on which they can lean.

Today

I will see where I am at
fault when I choose to deny
another person the integrity
to follow their own hearts'
desires and dreams.

Humility

So often we get angry and frustrated with those we love because they aren't "doing it our way." Who is to say "our way" is the right way? It creates more confusion than harmony when we try to change another's personality to meet our needs rather than theirs.

Usually, the best course to follow when we are distressed with someone close to us, is to redirect our thoughts and see where they might be right, for man has very limited omniscience.

It is important for us to realize that adding harmony, to any situation, will result in us finding our own serenity.

God help me to humble myself that I will realize that I am imperfect, too.

Today

I will think before I act.

Planning – Organizing

Before we can make any decision we must first think through all the options available.

Thinking seriously about our choices displays attitudes of sincere fairness, honesty, and integrity. It's when we react impulsively to situations, instead of responding appropriately to them, that we usually create more confusion, resentment, and disappointments.

Choices about life episodes, made without considering all the consequences, can cause resentment and animosity in our relationships.

Like the child who wants to go outside and play in the rain. The mother reacts to the child's request before thinking and immediately says, "No!" Maybe she makes this abrupt decision because she doesn't want him to catch cold.

If she thought through the situation more carefully, however, she might have considered the child's pleasure and handed him a raincoat and an umbrella. Besides, the rain probably would have let up after a bit, anyway. For no situation lasts forever, not even rain.

"Responding" to situations is to be accountable and fair.

Today

I realize that in order to see more clearly the beauty of God's Grace, I need to uncover and discard any personal resentments and harmful conflicts in my relationships.

Acceptance

The world and its workings seem to function all around us with no pity or applause when we are struggling or succeeding at the game of life. Rivers and streams still flow, ocean tides still rise and fall, the sun still comes up at dawn and sets at eventide, and man's business arena succeeds or fails without us.

All circumstances in life are a part of God's plan to refine the soul. Any dissatisfaction we have within exists because we have created the unhappiness.

We "as humans" have the right to live free from internal destruction. And we "can" when we clearly understand that we, alone, have formed the barriers of self delusion which keep us in bondage to self-pity. In order to overcome the illusion that we are more powerful than God, we must choose to recognize that God is in control of our lives. Only then is it possible to rebuild our dreams on a foundation that is sure to be filled with success.

Today

I will start to uncover my emotions so I may live in greater peace with God, myself, and others.

✤Emotions

There is no pain more hurtful than emotional pain. Along the way we are bound to experience some emotional discomfort whether the level of pain is overwhelming or subtle in its intensity.

If we don't walk through our pain, we will continue to experience the same anguish over and over and over again, until we finally get a real understanding of our behavior and attitude towards our emotions.

When we acknowledge our sorrows and accept them as our own, instead of blaming others, then we are on the path to recovery. We surmount emotional pain by facing it head on.

We will experience great joy and peace on the other side of the mountain of pain, but we have to conquer the mountain first. It is then that we gain freedom.

Today

Passion will be my guide.

✣Passion

Fear clouds our perception of the truth. It's the nature of this beastly emotion. Overwhelming in its appearance, it draws all of our attention and distorts reality, sometimes beyond recall.

In contrast, love casts out all fear. The passion of love's grace will open up our hearts and minds to new and challenging panoramas. When we are guided by love, the view of any situation is altered and we see clearly God's hand upon our lives.

Passion: this joyous emotion allows us to feel love and understanding for all things and all people. To understand, instead of trying to be understood, should be our motto.

We must always be cautious when the ghost of fear confronts us. The only thing we should ever be afraid of is "fear itself".

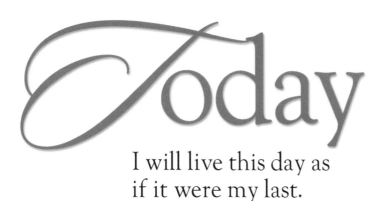

Today

I will live this day as
if it were my last.

❧One day at a time.

Unleash your creativity by living this day as if it were your last. Our fragile souls need stimuli that will inspire hope, love, and freedom from worry. Seize the moment and let your imagination run wild. For what if this really was your last day on this earth? Would you have accomplished all you desired, all you set out to do?

What is it you seek? Is it love? Is it fame, or wealth, or travel or peace? If it is one of these or even something else, go for it! Auntie Mame, in the book and movie of the same name, summed it up best when she said, "Life is a banquet, what a pity most people are starving to death."

I'll always remember the wise old woman who stood in front of me at the checkout counter of my neighborhood supermarket. She must have been in her eighties and her poor old body was bent over with age. Yet despite her physical circumstances, she proudly thanked the clerk, smiled at him and said, "It's a good day today! I'm alive!"

She knew the real secret to life! She was living for today, not yesterday, not tomorrow, but today. So, no matter what day, month, or year it is, once it is gone, it is gone. We can never reclaim the past. Therefore, make the most of today! For perhaps it is really all we have left.

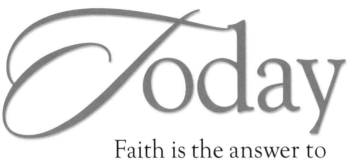

Today

Faith is the answer to childlike happiness.

❧Laughter – Smile

Children bring happiness to us with their quick wit and their bright smiles. We could be having the worst day of our life when we encounter a young child who "simply smiles or giggles" and suddenly our burdens are lifted. We immediately stop addressing our own problems and see where we can add to the light of the child's laughter.

It's not an easy task to just let go of our difficulties. The truth is, however, that worrying about our problems only places more stress on us than necessary.

What a relief it is when we can have enough faith that our needs are being met and finally believe that things are just the way they are supposed to be at that given moment.

We have less anxiety in our lives when we can become like children and, "simply smile."

Today

I realize that the opportunities for a fulfilling career are manifested by my own attitude.

✿ Attitude

Grey dawns begin to appear more frequently when we lose genuine interest in our daily work. Any glimmer of hope we had for ourselves evaporates before our eyes when our only reason for working is the paycheck.

But how do we keep the fire of enthusiasm burning when the tasks at hand are so monotonous? An assembly worker might bring an iPod to work with inspiring music and audio books. A housewife could dance to music while she dusts the shelves, feeds the children, or vacuums.

A taxicab driver might interview his passengers on "success and what it meant to them," and then write a book about it. When our imagination is fired, anything is possible. Any occupation we hold can be challenging if we let our creativity unfold and come alive.

Today

I will see how other people's lives
give me an opportunity to work
on my own imperfections.

Inventory

Sometimes we are critical and judgmental of other people's behaviors. What we must understand is that in seeing the behaviors of others, we make choices about our own lives.

Our search for truth must start first within ourselves. We have to first look at our own personal happiness before we can move forward to face new challenges.

Obstacles on the road of happiness are not created by others but by our own perceptions. Studying and inventorying our own truths and values will give us insights that will help us achieve future goals and eliminate most of the judgmental detours.

It is only possible for us to mature and grow when we can identify our own faults. Sometimes we cannot recognize our character flaws until we see these same deficiencies in other people's character. Therefore, other peoples' defects of character allow us important opportunities to recognize and inventory our own shortcomings.

Today

I will let love be my guide.

✿|Love

Love is the greatest gift given to us by God. When love is felt in our lives, the path we have chosen seems smoother and freer. We feel there are no barriers in front of us. Anything we wish to accomplish seems easier and more attainable.

It's only when we forget about the love we share that we find ourselves stagnant and unforgiving. It's easy to get caught up in our daily tasks and overlook this precious gift of love.

"Love relationships" will always give us the courage we need to overcome the obstacles we face in our lives. Our personal strengths are revealed when we acknowledge love and its healing power.

Today

I realize the answers to all my problems are within my own consciousness. They will be revealed as long as I remain patient.

 Patience

Whirlwinds of life, including disgruntled family relationships, can cause us to lose our spiritual balance. When we build the foundation of our lives on the principles of love, patience, and tolerance, the less vulnerable we will be to the destructive powers of minor squabbles.

Every decision we make has an effect upon our lives as a whole. Sometimes we make mistakes and have to repair the damage. It's a part of life. But if we listen closely to our inner voice, we can avoid the fury of life's dangerous flames of selfish resentment. It is a lot simpler to extinguish a controlled campfire than it is to conquer a roaring conflagration caused by uncontrolled emotions.

We intuitively know when our lives are out of balance. Being aware of our own limitations helps us keep most situations in perspective. We are more able to resolve our problems "appropriately" when we slow down long enough to see how we can resolve our problems based on spiritual principles.

Today

I pray for God's presence in my life and that I am humble enough to be graced by His presence as I climb the ladder of success.

❧Faith

Behind every great man and woman is an unquestionable belief in the power of God.

Their belief in God led them into recognized positions of power and wealth throughout the world. Others followed them in their leadership. When they shared their ideas, they emphasized their belief in God.

They came to realize, through their incredible successes, that without God, they would never have been able to carry the message of hope to their dedicated followers.

Although these men and women garnered the riches of their successful lives through many different philosophies, they clearly understood that God had been their infinite source of wealth.

If we are to have love and serenity in our hearts, money in our pockets, and true mental and emotional freedom, we have to realize where true power comes from. That power is God.

Today

I will be transparent
long enough for someone
to see my pain and help
me walk through it.

Fellowship – Friendship

To trudge through the tunnel of doom alone is not only a frightening and lonely road, but is one that need not exist.

Sometimes we carry heavy burdens longer than necessary. What we might label as utter despair can often be translated into an opportunity to learn more about ourselves. Our fears are magnified when we face them alone. But if we humble ourselves enough to share our frustrations with another human being we immediately feel a sense of relief.

Shields of steel can protect us from bodily harm. But they do not suffice in times of loneliness and despair. We triumph over terror when we can let go of our phobias long enough to let someone touch us with their love.

Today

I will realize the
symmetry of life and
the perfection in which
it was born.

 Harmony - Balance

Beware of boredom and boundaries. Because of them, we fall to pieces in our minds. We create these boundaries and sometimes small stones of lethargy build themselves into boulders of fear and depression.

We mustn't blur our vision with listless hopelessness. Instead, we can break the habit of thinking the impossible by embarking upon a new idea when boredom takes over in our consciousness.

We should be like the ocean tide that rises and falls with ease. By flowing like the tide that sweeps away all before it, we can accept new challenges. By doing this we can do away forever with boundaries.

The beautiful and the bountiful are within us each moment of each day.

Today

I will remember to count my
blessings and bestow my kindness
upon those I know and meet.

⚘Gratitude

There are many chances throughout our day to better ourselves. A kind word or a generous thought towards a fellow worker, family member, or loved one can cause that person to respond in kind.

Gossip, resentments, talking, or just thinking maliciously about our friends and family can bring us nothing more than a bowl full of discord and unhappiness.

We must commit our loyalty to others by being generous toward them in thought, word, and deed. We cannot expect any person, place, or thing to help us begin taking benevolent actions. We must do it ourselves.

How do we accomplish this? We start each morning with a prayer and continue throughout the day with the same gratitude for life.

We experience a much greater joy when we realize that life itself is a blessing and that true happiness is discovered when we share our love and hope with others, instead of our judgments and criticisms.

Today

I will remember my
family and friends first,
for they are the foundation
on which my successes are built.

❧Service

We make certain decisions in our lives that lay the foundation for our future. If we are careful when choosing our direction, we will be amazed at the successes that follow our decisions.

We must always consider the health and welfare of our family, friends, professional associates, and partners when setting goals. We must come to realize that any success we gain that is based solely on "self" will fail.

We must decide to be of service first to others, then to ourselves, in order to produce harmony all around us. It is in the giving of ourselves that we lay down a solid foundation that is sure to succeed.

There is a network of sorts that exists among all of us. Our lives are intertwined with so many relationships it is impossible to succeed in life if we leave out the main ingredient: Love.

Today

I will take action in prayer, reminding myself that it is by changing my behaviors, not in changing others' actions, that I become happy, joyous, and free.

❧|Resentment – Anger

We often come across people who seem to "get the best of us." As much as we try to change our feelings towards those individuals, we fail. For some reason, we haven't let go of our anger and resentment towards them.

If we are to be happy, joyous, and free, we must find a way to change. Changing "our" actions is the key. The action best taken in these situations is prayer. Praying for others' health, happiness, and prosperity creates unity in all of our relationships.

We cannot change someone else, nor do we want to. Instead, we agree to disagree with these individuals and pray for ourselves and them. It's in the action of prayer that we learn more about true caring and understanding of others.

Our lives should not be bent on making another person understand how we feel. Instead, we should learn to have more compassion for their feelings. True freedom from anger is a direct result of action taken in prayer. It is not our job to change others but rather to change ourselves.

Today

I realize the power
of honesty.

❧Happiness

Dazzle them with your wit and you will be remembered. It's always a pleasure to be in the company of someone who just likes to laugh and has the gift to make others laugh as well. When we walk away from this sort of person, we feel relieved of our troubles.

Laughing at our own imperfections, failures, and misgivings deadens the sting of the sword. When we share with another our deepest secrets, our impediments lose the power that they wield over our attitudes. The darkness where our troubles have come to rest is then free to dissipate and gratitude can take their place.

We might say, "Why have we kept that a secret for so long, it wasn't all that bad?" It's important to become vulnerable with others. Honesty opens up doors to friendship, laughter, and real emotion.

Today

I will allow myself the right
to feel pain, past or present,
so that I may find my inner
light of hope and faith.

❧ Pain

We develop an inner calm when we allow ourselves to feel emotional pain. The sorrows of the past and present are real and must be addressed before freedom and joy can be experienced. Stuffing our grief in the corridors of our mind prohibits the soul from knowing the great joys of solace and relief.

The problem with most of us is that we have been taught from an early age to not feel or show our pain. The words, "It's going to be all right; Don't cry or be sad," ring in our ears from childhood.

But if we can re-examine certain sorrowful episodes and allow the pain to surface, the void created is replaced with happiness and love. Pain must be allowed to be felt and resolved before our imagination can be ignited and the door of success unlocked.

Today

I will displace one of
my shortcomings by taking
the opposite action of
my normal behavior.

Inventory

In all areas of our lives there is an opportunity for us to be loving and kind. Our actions from this day forward can determine the sort of person we wish to become. Habit, good or bad, is formed and developed by our actions.

Our shortcomings don't disappear merely by praying or willing them away. Instead, they are displaced by the seriousness of our daily efforts to remove them.

For example, if we have a tendency to be discourteous and angry on the highway towards other motorists, we can change our behavior by kindly waving to everyone we encounter until this "new habit" has replaced the old.

When we practice principles instead of constantly discussing and complaining about our difficulties, our problems are resolved. It's the living your way into right thinking, instead of thinking your way into right living that makes the difference.

Today

I will open up my heart and
let the love I have to share
pour out to those in need.

 Love

For you I'd tramp the swamplands
Thick as the Everglades
I'd weather the ice caps
On the coldest of days
For you I'd light a fire,
And cuddle up close
To listen to your dreams
Your poems and prose
There isn't anything
I wouldn't do,
If I knew you needed me
I'd be true.

Let us be an example by reaching out and caring for each other. We can brighten up the dullest days by letting go of our own problems and lending an ear to someone else's.

Love is received when we learn how to give.

Today

I will free myself from the weight of the world and start living in the light of a new day.

Habit – Behavior – Action

Twisted scores of limited visions and a torn heart to mend can leave us lingering in depression. Our home is in our hearts and our dreams begin in our minds.

We deprive ourselves of love and success by forming negative habits. We must take caution when we find ourselves in a place where the daily tasks are insurmountable.

Flexibility in everyday living promotes peace of mind. Without serenity we can't see the trees through the forest. We must temper our minds to melt useless thoughts and create more positive ones on a daily basis.

If we are tenacious at this process, we will begin to see the light at the end of the tunnel. And the closer we get to the light, the brighter it becomes.

Today

I truly believe that my dreams will come true if I work for them.

Visions – Success

Our hopes and dreams are built on faith. Our fantasies can become realities, in time, if we are willing to take certain steps to achieve our goals.

Each day we must work toward the dream or the dream will not come true. There is no such thing as gaining something for nothing. Every action has a reaction. So, if it is happiness we are looking for, we must work every day towards achieving it. In time, our actions will become second nature and we will "be happy."

It's like learning to ride a bicycle. At first we must make a concerted effort to balance ourselves in order to move forward without falling. In time, after many attempts, we achieve the art of bicycle riding. No longer do we have to think about it, we just do it.

Our dreams are "developed" in the same way.

Today

I will seek my independence
by caring for others through prayer,
kindness, and thoughtfulness.

❧Honesty – Truth

Honesty is the true path to independence. The respect we have for ourselves begins with understanding the dreams of others while keeping our minds focused on our own lives. When we are able to respect others then we can become respectful of ourselves.

Although independence seems like a simple feat for some of us, some of the time, in reality we can only grasp its true meaning when we allow ourselves to be unselfishly considerate towards others.

But we can be selfish even when we think our behavior is considerate. That is when we give somebody else the right to be themselves only when we can gain some sort of satisfaction from our benevolent conduct.

Independence is received when we are altruistic in thought and behavior.

Today

I will have enough courage
to keep my eyes focused on
my own personal growth.

❧Expectations

Criticizing the actions of others is a detour towards realizing our own shortcomings. Our judgment of others only sweeps our personal character flaws under the carpet. In addition, more defects will manifest themselves in our behaviors when we lower our standards and become the judge and jury of other people's lives.

It is not our job in life to work out someone else's problems. It is our responsibility, however, to learn from our own mistakes, admit our faults, and grow in the light of faith.

We cannot succeed in life when we are too busy worrying about other people's problems. Our focus should be directed solely towards our own personal achievement and growth.

When we can accept ourselves and grow from our misgivings and failures, then we become free to venture and succeed at anything we want in life.

Today

I have peace in my
life. I am no longer at war
with myself or others.

Fear

We so often fight to keep our job, our respect, our loved one's attention, even our sanity. What we overlook is that this war is self-defeating. One of the greatest obstacles we will ever have to overcome, in our life's journey, is our own neurotic and undisciplined thinking.

It's what is called the "individual mental medley competition." There is only one player in this mental battle and it is us, alone.

When we let go of the need for emotional applause from our friends and family, we let go of the main reason to fight. We no longer live in fear. The relationship we have with ourselves and with others can be abundantly peaceful and full of joy, if we can simply follow a few rules. They are:

A.   Give first, always
B.   Love unconditionally, always
C.   Be of service, always
D.   Act unselfishly, always

These are just basic guidelines that we can utilize to lessen our own mental and emotional battles.

Today

I realize the benefits of true humility. I can admit my mistakes freely, realizing that love is re-established in my relationships when I am willing to humble myself when I am wrong.

Resentment – Anger

Children are taught from an early age to apologize when they have done something wrong. Sometimes young people are even made to apologize for behaviors and attitudes, not knowing that their conduct was selfish and inconsiderate. In time, children turn into adults.

It is then that they start to justify their actions to protect their integrity. "I'm sorry," can be the hardest words to express. We might think we demean ourselves when we have to admit our errors, especially when we believe that the other person's actions are inappropriate as well.

It is an act of bravery when we can assess our own attitudes, see where our faults lie, and apologize promptly to whomever we have harmed. Holding grudges and resentments leads nowhere. Worse, it corrupts our serenity.

There is nothing like a good, "I'm sorry," to clear the air in our relationships. It relieves the tension that resentment and bitter feelings can cause between people. Sincere apologies will also begin the healing process that is necessary for spiritual growth.

Today

I will pray for all those who are in need and I will reach out my hand to someone who is less fortunate than I am.

Service

Tears should well up in our eyes when we see a homeless person or family standing on a street corner with a sign that reads "Will Work for Food."

We should recognize that the exact same spot in which they stand, or one like it, might one day be occupied by our own children or loved one. Perhaps, it already is.

Everyday we notice many indigents on the streets. We quickly pass by them while driving our cars, sometimes hoping they won't make eye contact because of our guilt. We then proceed to drive on, forgetting them entirely, until the same scene is repeated somewhere else.

It is our responsibility as fellow human beings to assist the spiritually poor, through these, their darkest days. For by sharing our hope and showing our concern for the sick and the downtrodden, we allow a small ray of light to enter into their weathered souls.

We can plant seeds of faith in these weak souls through prayer, charity, and love. Moreover, we feel the power of God's light growing stronger in our own hearts when we are generous. The Indigo Girls, the musicians, describe it best when they say, "If we have a care for the world we have a gift to bring."

Today

I will be grateful for the small
voice that guides my life.

❧Gratitude

We've all had extremely difficult and trying periods in our lives. During these intervals we sometimes feel hopeless, helpless, and lost.

Every waking moment our minds are consumed by a fruitless search for the "perfect answer" to our dilemmas. So much concentrated effort is expended on "what to do" that our feelings get lost in the midst of our intellect.

When we experience trials and tribulations, writing a gratitude list will, without a doubt, stop us so abruptly in our tracks that we are more able to focus on the present instead of the past or future.

When we stop worrying and start thanking God for His presence and praying for His will, the "perfect answer" will appear. Why worry if you pray and why pray if you worry?

The answer to our problems is not found when we chaotically search for them. Instead, our solutions are revealed when we are quiet long enough to hear in the stillness, that follows, God's whisper.

Today

I choose to associate with the
friends and lovers who support
me in all my endeavors.

❧Relationships

Relationships have a tremendous amount of influence on our lives. They can either inspire and guide us or corrupt and mislead us. We must, therefore, be cautious when choosing our business partners, acquaintances, associates, and especially, friends and lovers.

Any form of negativity, in any part of any relationship, can devastate our emotional, spiritual, or mental health. We must ask ourselves these questions about our friends and lovers.

Are they inspiring or corrupting? Are they supportive and loving or are they demeaning and full of jealousy? And lastly, are they growing and helping us to grow?

Although all relationships aren't 100% perfect 100% of the time, we must seek out the pros and eliminate the cons (as in artist).

We all learn from relationships, good and bad. Our level of achievement will accelerate and our pathways to success will become smoother if we can associate with people who are positive for us.

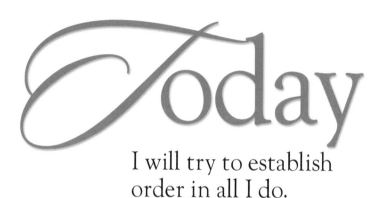

Today

I will try to establish
order in all I do.

Harmony – Balance

Organization is a quality we all admire. It would be very frustrating for us if, when we went shopping for food, clothing, or practically anything, we found not rows of neatly arranged goods, but mammoth mounds of unsorted items. Fortunately for most of us this is not the case.

Store owners have learned that it is financially unfeasible to be unorganized. And so it is with each of us. We must possess a certain amount of orderliness in order to accomplish our goals. If we didn't organize our lives appropriately, the bills wouldn't be paid, the children wouldn't get to school on time, and meals wouldn't be prepared.

The quality of our own organizational competence is best portrayed by the amount of "time we waste" searching for misplaced items. The way in which we develop the poetry of our lives will have a direct bearing on the amount of stress we possess.

Life is so much simpler and more pleasant when we are able to organize it.

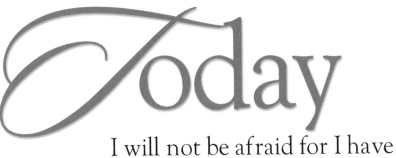

Today

I will not be afraid for I have
faith in life's perfection.

Faith

Faith is best defined as believing in something you can't see, feel, hear, or smell. It is an intuition that everything is okay no matter what the circumstances.

Faith is not religion. Faith is a soul-searched insight that believes in life's perfection at all times. If we don't have faith, how do we get it?

Usually faith is found as we walk through our fears. Some of these fears are poverty, criticism, illness, and death.

When we take "the step of faith," by trusting God, we are able to love and cherish every circumstance in our lives.

Enlightenment about God's plan is revealed suddenly sometimes and sometimes it seems like His plan is failing. But, in order for faith to remain a force in our lives, we must nurture our relationship with God through prayer, no matter what we think.

Today

I realize that growth comes
from letting go of my pride long
enough for me to face my fears.

Pride

Our resentments will follow any of life's conditions which are not equal to or better than our justified standards of living. Usually, what surfaces from our anger is not the pain we are experiencing but our indignant nature as our ego is challenged.

Pride is the major culprit of our resentments. We soften the core of our anger by acknowledging the origin of its existence. The root of all anger is fear. As we overcome fear of ourselves and others, we have less reason for battle.

Our indignant nature leaves us and resentment surfaces rarely when we face our fears instead of protecting them with our pride.

Today

I will seek success by
serving others.

✦ Service

Success is a by-product of service work for others. Selfish behavior, including the "I want this or that" syndrome, can only delay the fulfillment of our dreams.

We can only receive back what we give to the world. So if along our journey we step on the toes of others while trying to realize our goals, we risk losing the love and respect of those around us.

We must face the reality that the main reason for our desire to achieve success should be to share it with people along our way. Without love there is only spiritual emptiness, loneliness, and unhappiness.

Our desires for success, realized in our service work and love for others, will be one of the most fulfilling emotions we will ever experience. When we feel sidetracked by life's setbacks, we can immediately change our attitudes about them by remembering that life is richer when we are serving others. We will always find peace, love, and harmony on the other side of service.

Today

I can succeed because I include
my loved ones in my journey.

❧Fellowship – Friendship

From the moment we are brought into this world until the day we draw our last breath, our minds, bodies, and souls are nourished by the score of friends and family members who touch us.

Allowing ourselves to foster an attitude of self-reliance resembles the characteristics of someone suffering from self-delusion. John Donne, the sixteenth century poet, described it best when he wrote, "No man is an Iland, entire of it selfe; every man is a peece of the continent, a part of the maine."

Or like the man who decided to conquer the highest peak of Mt. Whitney alone. Upon reaching the top he found himself exhausted and freezing to death with no one near to share either his triumph for his successful climb or to give him aid in this hour of need.

As we march through the peaks and valleys of our lives, we experience much greater satisfaction when we allow friends and family to share our journey.

Today

I will work to change old habits
so that I can achieve happiness
in my present-day life.

Habit – Behavior – Action

Our childhood haunts our adult life in many ways. Too much love; not enough love; beaten or spoiled; emotionally over-protected or emotionally starved by parents who were selfish and self-centered in nature.

There is no medical or psychological therapy available that can turn the pages back and reconstruct a childhood. It is impossible to turn time backwards.

Our adult behavior patterns are usually a result of the treatment we received as a child. We can find great freedom when we are willing to accept, learn, change, and grow from our awareness of our past and present experiences.

A thorough inventory of our lives helps us to recognize our faults and begin to understand and change them. If we are persistent in our endeavors, we will achieve inner growth and become increasingly happy.

On the other hand, if we do not make an effort to grow, we will eventually fall back into old behavior patterns and our lives will be empty and unfulfilling.

Today

I will realize there is wisdom in every moment and joy in every second if I allow every experience in my life, to be a spiritual experience.

Growth

Not one day passes that we aren't given the opportunity to grow up emotionally and better ourselves spiritually. Yet, often we emit a loud sigh of relief when it is over.

We try to forget the tumultuous day that has just passed and pray for a better tomorrow. It seems strange that we wish for days to be done with when our time is limited here on earth.

What if this day were our last day to live? Would we be satisfied with our final actions?

As we absorb this wisdom, we should offer up a prayer of gratitude as blissful dreams possess us instead of a sigh of relief.

Today

I will make a sincere effort to
laugh at my mistakes, smile when
someone passes me by, and reach
out with gratitude for life.

❧Laughter – Smile

Being a part of the crowd, one of the guys or gals, is a desire of every human being. How we behave socially can either draw people closer to us or push them away from us.

If we are boastful, egotistical, angry, selfish, or glum our friendships will be limited. However, if we are complimentary, humble, happy, of service, active and purposeful our successes will be uncanny.

One effective way of attracting friends lies in the power of a smile. Our own lives are enriched when we reach out to others with a sincere appreciation of their existence.

We've all been around a little baby who's happy and giggly. As we observe this baby's contentment we feel a sense of belonging and a simple gratitude for life. There is nothing else we could do but to smile back at the child.

If a child can attract people to him just by smiling and laughing, the same principle can be applied in our own lives. We've all heard the saying, "laugh and the world laughs with you, weep and you weep alone."

Today

I will focus on the magnificence
of each moment.

❧One Day at a Time

So often we let our "undisciplined" minds rule our destiny and, in so doing, we create a living hell for ourselves. Too easily we complicate our every-day tasks with negative thoughts. Thus, reality becomes overwhelming when our minds in this pessimistic state, takes control of our lives.

To find the beauty that lies within each moment, we must step outside, the inside of our thoughts, and look to experience whatever is right in front of us.

All our goals have a purpose and can be realized. When we can concentrate on the present moment we lessen the chance of our stumbling on the path of success. Keeping our attention focused solely on what is at hand, while charting our life's course in the stillness of our mind, assists us in enjoying the beauty and grace of every step we take along our journey.

Today

I realize that true wisdom is
born out of every adversity
I have encountered.

Adversity

Life's daily struggles have a definite purpose in our lives. They do not exist merely to make us crazy. Instead pain exists to enlighten us; to make us aware of the powerful gifts God has placed before us.

These gifts include faith, patience, tolerance, virtue and love. If we never toiled over anything, nothing would be sown.

Hardships, placed in their proper perspective, can become the true bearers of wisdom. And from wisdom, we discover that God's spiritual armor and His presence are eminently more productive and satisfying.

When adversity is manifested and we overcome the battles of life by relying on God and His wisdom our purpose for living is clarified. Adversities appear in our lives to help us find our true spiritual identity.

Today

I will not hold back any
kind thoughts. Instead, I
will shower everyone I meet
with an encouraging word,
a sense of hope, and a smile.

Change – Principles

One of the most treasured gifts we have as human beings is the ability to give of ourselves without expecting something in return.

We all exchange presents on our birthdays. It is traditional to do so. But what really can touch another person's heart are the intangible things we can offer our friends and families. These gifts are such things as encouragement, love, hope, and a kind word of appreciation.

To proffer these treasures to others on a daily basis can truly alter our own lives. For when we give freely of ourselves, we are rewarded tenfold.

We feel a tremendous sense of thankfulness and a warm glow inside when we share ourselves unconditionally. Our souls are filled with a strange calm and the burdens of the world are lifted when we practice the principles of giving.

Today

I will dream the impossible and commit to the possible.

❧|Dreams

We all have dreams and we all wish for them to come true. Most often though in the darkest recesses of our minds, we set limits of deep uncertainty which block the path to our desires.

Goals can seldom be achieved when doubt is clogging our minds. It is only by commitment and total faith that we are capable of acquiring whatever it is we have dreamed of possessing.

Each day we must reach for the sky in all our endeavors. We must hold fast to the idea of a limitless universe, remembering always to give more to others than we expect in return.

If we do this every day, we will be filled with more joy and satisfaction than we could ever have imagined.

Today

I will surrender my pride
and open up my heart so
that I may find peace and
joy in my own life.

Pride

Pride is one of the biggest obstacles we must overcome to find the truth about ourselves. Our egos build walls which separate us from God, the world, and all people that live in it. When we are in conflict with our fellowmen chances are our pride has set the boundaries.

It is only when we surrender and let go of our pride that we gain self-acceptance and self-worth. Slowly, over time, by trusting God and not our finite perceptions, we can learn to share our lives with others openly and become a part of theirs.

When we give up our pride, the walls that separate us from God and the rest of the world will tumble down.

Today

I will believe in me.

Choice

Sometimes the problems we are confronted with in life seem too overwhelming for us to face alone. This is especially true if we decide to seek advice, opinions, information, and even extracurricular data from others, rather than to have faith in God's ability to guide our judgments.

Although this strategy may work for a period of time, in the long run it can be very destructive if we have eliminated our feelings in the midst of data based on other people's opinions. It is impossible to make our choices based on someone else's experience or knowledge without God's help.

No human being will ever have enough information about us to solve our living problems. Our solutions await us when we search within ourselves and seek God earnestly without any reservations.

When we are fearless before God we will find that we, ourselves, always have the best answer.

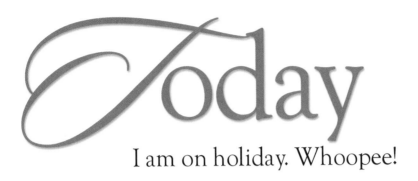

Today

I am on holiday. Whoopee!

Harmony – Balance

Most of us have two lives. One is defined as "Work" and the other as 'Vacation.' We would all like to be "always on vacation." It's a place where we can relax, unwind, and release ourselves from our worries and problems.

The truth is plain though. "Vacation" and "Work" are just labels we, ourselves, have attached to a controlled time frame.

Our careers, whether they are occupations such as housewife, salesperson, accountant, doctor, or beautician, are "our lives" at their best. We have chosen our paths and now we can enjoy the pleasures of our choices.

If we just remove the assigned label "work" which we have created for our occupations, what may appear as work can be mentally transformed and become recreation. "Work" and "Vacation" then become synonymous and we enjoy unity and contentment in everything we do.

Today

I realize that my vision is only
limited by my perceptions.

Visions – Success

As we observe our lives and our environment we develop our own unique perceptions of them. There are some people who would look at a millionaire and truly believe they could never achieve the same amount of monetary success. There are others who might have the opposite view.

These perceptions of people, places, and things are created in our own minds. We limit our successes by thinking only in one-dimensional spheres. Once we have formed an opinion on a certain idea, these then become habits which are hard to break.

Would you say the glass is half full or half empty? Or would you, or could you abandon your physical perception and imagine the glass overflowing under an eternal tap?

How we see our lives is how we will live them. We create our own distorted perception of success when we rely on the world's perspectives. On the other hand, if we allow God to guide our minds, we will find success in every area of our lives.

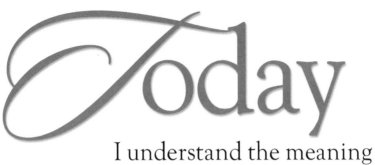

Today

I understand the meaning
of true humility.

❧|Humility

It is difficult to uncover and see the real truth that lies in the hollows and clefts of our minds and souls. We rely too heavily on the outside world to fill the void that is left inside us after emotional tragedies.

Our faith tends to dwindle in the midst of any difficulty we may encounter. But our prayers for help are answered if we humbly ask God for His help and direction.

Through prayer our visions are fortified. Prayer helps us to recognize that tribulations exist to enlighten and strengthen our wisdom of life itself. It is only in prayer that we come to realize that our mortal sufferings are as nothing compared to the magnificent universe and the hereafter.

In every adversity lies the seed of equal or greater benefits.

Today

I will realize that fear is just a stepping stone to freedom.

Honesty – Truth

If we are to become happy, joyous, and free, then we must first learn the value of honesty and self-respect.

It is only when we intentionally or unintentionally deceive ourselves or others that our freedom is limited. Because of our lies, we are driven to cover up the real truth.

We must learn not to avoid our fears, but instead, learn to walk through them by trusting God. By aquiring "God centered" coping skills we are able to conquer fear of being honest with ourselves and others. Once we are spiritually equipped, we receive self-respect and dignity.

Today

Physical fitness will
be a priority in my life as
I realize how important
it is to be healthy.

Appearance – Physical Fitness

Our sound physical health is of primary importance in all of our lives. If we neglect the body, our mental, emotional, and spiritual capacities are hindered.

Eating properly, exercising daily, taking mini-vacations from work, and right skin care not only keep our physical body in sound condition but lets us more clearly concentrate on our goals.

Any exercise, including jogging, walking, aerobics, swimming, bicycling, yoga, or just stretching assists the body to eliminate dead cells and aids in the process of rejuvenation.

Mini-vacations to the beaches, mountains or lakes, purifies the mind, and relieves unwanted stresses. Eating properly and taking vitamins also help to prevent the common cold and flu. We all feel better when we are physically fit.

Today

I will be a part of my own plan.

❧Planning – Organizing

Every decision we make in life affects our personal well being. It is our responsibility to make choices that benefit not only us, but others as well.

When we are obsessed to acquire material possessions we might have a momentary feeling of triumph, but that is just what it is, momentary. We must have merit in the choices we make before we can enjoy the benefits we receive from our altruistic decisions.

The surest way to achieve our goal is to plan wisely, then take action, being careful not to hurt anyone in the process.

We will experience more joy along the path of success if we stop believing that it is only the final destination that will bring us happiness. Contentment comes to us when we participate in the design of our dreams at every turn in the road.

Every dream house is first an idea, then a sketch, then a construction project, then a home where we live. Each step of our life's mission has many facets. Profoundly enough, our lives can be lived and built in the same way.

Today

I understand that my
success is strengthened by
changing old destructive
behaviors and sustaining
my positive moral nature.

Habit – Behavior – Action

Winning at the game of life takes goal setting and daily actions. We will never realize our dreams if we believe that our wishes for success will just materialize without persistent step-taking.

There are very few individuals who gamble with fortune successfully. To become true champions at the game of life we must take the first step by incorporating positive thoughts and action into our daily behavior.

When we become aware of every attribute or fault that we possess, we begin to recognize the power behind true consciousness. We can then, cleanse the soul of its past and put into action a plan for a new life.

By acknowledging our weaknesses, as well as our strengths, we are able to map out a strategy that will bring us the serenity we have been searching for.

Today

I will not take for granted
the ones I love. They are
what feed my soul.

Fellowship – Friendship

Our lives were not meant to be hidden in shallow pools of darkness, instead, they were meant to be enveloped in folds of eternal light. We are not destined to exist alone.

When we share our hopes and experiences with each other our lives are enriched tenfold. We end up alone only when we shut out the force which nurtures our will for living. That force is love.

Without love for each other we would perish. Like a budding rose that needs water and sunlight for nourishment, we must have fellowship to blossom and grow.

Love has no boundaries and can touch even the angriest of souls. Our insecurities are overcome and a new freedom is born in us when we can embrace the supernatural healing we experience after we have learned to love others unconditionally.

Today

I will take the step
of faith.

Faith

Having the ability to transform our fears into faith is the greatest tool man has been given. It is the iridescent candle midst the darkness of the soul.

So often fear prohibits the light of faith to overcome the power it wields over us. We block the path of enlightenment when we shut the door on faith.

Love and beauty await the traveler on the other side of the unknown. Yet, most of us often miss this Grace because we are too afraid of what new challenges, joys, or sorrows lie ahead.

Although we way not realize it today, our lives will have challenges and sorrows that will always turn out to be for our benefit.

Today

I understand that my
attitude will determine
whether or not I will
be present.

Inventory

Once we have experienced the ominous and precious power of living our lives one day at a time our souls will never again settle for anything less. Psychic pain and emotional suffering, however, will always precede this wisdom.

Our defects of character are magnified in times of despair rather than in the times when we are complacent living our life surrounded by creature comforts. We absolutely need great emotional setbacks so we don't consider ourselves perfect and become arrogantly judgmental of others.

Enlightenment in our daily lives is experienced in greater measure when we can honestly and frequently spot check our attitudes and motives in all circumstances. Life is too precious not to confront our inner conflicts and remove the obstacles that block us from experiencing the omnipotent and beautiful presence of God.

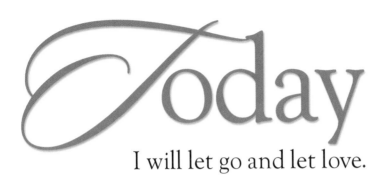

Today

I will let go and let love.

❧Love

Blessed are those who are humble enough to acknowledge that life is filled with temporary moments of heightened emotions and that love is the force that conquers these negative forces.

Our lives will continuously have triumphs and tribulations. Every experience we encounter in life teaches us to let go of our fears and trust in God's power.

Those of us who master the fury of uncontrolled emotion, which sometimes bursts forth in our relationships with others, will enjoy a much happier, freer life.

It is not our destiny to have to constantly overcome daily setbacks. On the contrary, we should be free to lead our lives in a peaceable and productive manner. To accomplish this, we must let go of our pride and let the love inside us surface.

As we practice the principle of forgiveness, we will experience a breath of renewed life reaching straight through to our very souls.

Today

I will realize the power that comes with compromise.

❧Relationships

Compromise is important in every relationship. There will always be differences of opinions, values, and ethics between men and women.

When we get into conflict with each other, our goal, as human beings seeking God's perfect and pleasing will, is to formulate a plan of action that will have peaceful results. There is always more than one way to tackle an unpleasant situation and we should recognize this truth.

If we are looking for a fight, we will find it. If we are hoping to achieve serenity, we will compromise and consider all options without hesitation.

It is without a doubt more important for us to find grace and safety than to constantly foment indignation in both ourselves and others. We lose respect when we resist the opportunity to compromise.

We gain much greater satisfaction when we realize our goals with the least amount of opposition and battle.

Today

I will open up my heart
and help those I can. For it is
through helping others that
I help myself.

Service

We have no time for worry in our lives. Each day is given to us by God that we may learn more about love. For it is in the love that we share and the trials we conquer that we gather strength and courage.

The more we wallow in self-pity, the less we are able to recognize what obstacles we have already surmounted. Each experience teaches us something valuable.

For wasn't it when we were depressed and lonely that we learned humility and how to open up our hearts to others? And wasn't it when we were happy and prosperous that we were able to share with others hope and faith?

Therefore, every life experience, regardless of how we label it, teaches us to let go of our fears and get closer to God and others.

Today

I will begin to heal myself in the
areas of anger and inner conflict.

Resentment – Anger

There are always two explanations for conflicts that exist in our relationships with others. Unfortunately it is very difficult for us to see the opposing point of view when we are experiencing confrontation. We usually, out of fear, resolve to incriminate the other side in order to defend our own behavior.

It's easier for us to be right than to admit we have any part in the argument we are having with someone else. We must remember this: the one who joins the fight is just as guilty as the one who starts it.

But how do we release ourselves from this destructive conduct of blaming others to justify our own needs? A simple plan of action is to be honest enough to admit that we aren't always right and then admit to ourselves that we usually act out of fear in confrontational situations.

Honesty, open-mindedness, and willingness to accept the fact that we might be wrong, can usually resolve our inner conflict. By nurturing ourselves and healing the inner anger we will no long have reason for battle.

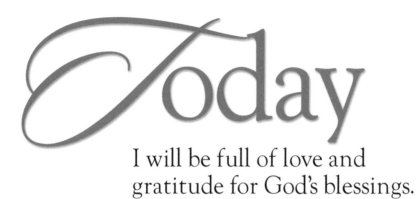

Today

I will be full of love and
gratitude for God's blessings.

⊰⊱Gratitude

It's hard to have a heart full of love and gratitude and at the same time have a belly full of fear and anger. In life there is nothing predictable. Each day is a new challenge and if we don't grow, we will spiral backwards into old emotional habits.

It's easier to hang on to old behavior patterns because they are so familiar and in some cases, worked for many years. To change, we must give up any fear that we are losing something.

When one door closes, another one opens. If we set our eyes on what has been freely given to us by God, instead of bewailing that which we don't have, we can greet each day with more serenity.

For total serenity we must accept our lives just as they are; nothing more, nothing less.

Today

I will be aware of
God's true path for my life.
I will always seek Him
when I am confronted
with worldly temptations.

❧ Happiness

God provides us with the strength and the courage to acknowledge and overcome all circumstances that leave us feeling empty and alone inside.

Some temptations seem harmless at first. We must be wary when confronted with another man's prepackaged happiness. For happiness is an inside job and can only be nurtured when we first become aware of the voids we have created.

Once we have acknowledged the truth about ourselves we can overcome our discontent by reaching out to God and asking Him to guide us again.

In addition, illusory temptations that provide only momentary pleasure can be so subtle in their deception that if we are not connected to God, we will fall prey to their inevitable destruction.

Today

I will remember that
change is not growing
towards perfection, but
is itself, a form of perfection.

❧Acceptance

To enjoy the beauty and grace that each day brings us, we must let go of our standards, schedules, and expectations. We begin to enjoy peace of mind when we accept each moment of our lives as perfect.

Every day we can anticipate change. It is a primary element that remains constant in all areas of our lives. Learning to let change unfold naturally gives us a greater sense of peace.

If we consider that God created us perfect it can only prove that we live in a perfect world when we are connected to Him.

Today

I will recognize that using positive sayings can lessen life's struggles.

⚜Attitude

The positive effect of written and verbal affirmations can lighten the heavy burdens we carry. Without inspiration our negativity can send us spiraling endlessly downward into a pit of despondency and despair.

Such quotes as: "Easy does it"; "Patience is a virtue"; "One day at a time"; "Let go and let God"; are invaluable to us when we feel life's difficulties are too heavy to bear.

If we take the time to instill these proverbs, or others like them, in our minds, we can enjoy a changed perspective.

We may never reach "attitude perfection." However, our troubles are endured with much greater grace and are often eased when we incorporate these small words of wisdom into our minds.

Today

I will rest my faith completely
on the living God who will
always be near me and take
care of all my needs.

❧ Visions – Success

Icy snowcaps upon mammoth mountains are so treacherous that it seems impossible to battle the terrain to reach the top. Yet the miracle of nature melts the snow and ice. We rest, gather our resources, and continue on our journey.

Once we are on the true path of success, which is spiritual by virtue of our humanity, we are called to be faithful. We risk our identities as God's blessed children when we deny His promise to strengthen and encourage us as we walk with Him onto the end.

Our inability to weather our fears should be an indication to us that we must overcome this fright or lose our souls in a tumultuous avalanche.

Once we have decided to take this journey, we must realize that for us to give up hope can destroy our will for happiness and serenity.

Today

I'll remember that patience is a virtue.

❧|Patience

Let us not depend on another person's happiness for our own serenity. We will never reach the heights of unlimited success by expecting others to applaud our achievements. Expectations bring more sorrow than happiness for most of us.

The unconditional tolerance and patience we expect from ourselves should be the same attitudes we express towards our friends and family.

We feel at peace within our own souls when we allow ourselves the freedom to let the world around us continue to rotate without expecting anything in return.

Today

I will visualize that my hopes
and dreams are only as distant
from reality as I wish them to
be. Today, I will start working on
making my dreams come true.

❧Visions – Success

"What do you want to be when you grow up?" The adult asks the child. The child replies, "I want to be a fireman." Another child exclaims, "A doctor," and a third blurts out, "I want to be president."

It isn't human nature to want to fail. We have never heard a child, or even an adult, express an overwhelming desire to be poverty-stricken or lead a life full of fear.

Yet, as we grow older we found that our childhood dreams never materialized. Instead, they have been pushed back to the inner recesses of our minds due to the need to concentrate on tackling the problems of everyday living. Schedules and responsibilities had supplanted the vision we had for a rosy future.

To realize our youthful ambitions we must never give up. We must nurture our inner strengths with courage and never lose faith in ourselves.

When we begin to feel that our dreams may never come true is the very moment we must press on with the persistence and faith of that young child.

Our visions of success are still alive within us. We only need to acknowledge them and work harder to make them become a reality.